Water

Where Does It Come From? Where Does It Go?

Paul Humphrey

Photography by Chris Fairclough

W

FRANKLIN WATTS

This edition 2003

Franklin Watts
96 Leonard Street
London
EC2A 4XD

Franklin Watts Australia
45-51 Huntley Street
Alexandria
NSW 2015

Planning and production by Discovery Books
Editors: Tamsin Osler, Samantha Armstrong
Designer: Ian Winton
Art Director: Jonathan Hair
Illustrators: Stuart Trotter, Raymond Turvey
Commissioned photography: Chris Fairclough

A CIP catalogue record for this book is available from the British Library

Dewey Decimal Classification: 628.1

ISBN: 0 7496 5254 3

Printed in Malaysia

Photographs:
Beamish The North of England Open Air Museum: 25b;
Severn Trent Water: 16, 23, 24, 25a, 26b, 27a, 27b;
Tony Stone Images: 5 (Timothy Shonnard).

Acknowledgements
Franklin Watts would like to thank Severn Trent Water Ltd
for its help in the production of this book.

Severn Trent Water

Contents

Turn on the tap

What's the most precious thing in your house – the television and video? the stereo? the computer? Actually it is something you probably don't think of as valuable at all. It's always there when you need it. All you have to do is turn on a tap and there it is – fresh, clean water.

Every day we need water for drinking, washing and cooking. We use it at school, in offices and in factories. But where does our water come from? And what happens to the water when we pull out the plug and it washes down the plughole?

Waste water from toilets is also washed
away from our homes. Where does it go?
How do we dispose of dirty water
without harming the environment?

Water companies supply our water.
They clean it, treat it and supply it to
our homes. They also take it away when
we have used it. They clean it, treat it
and return it to the rivers or the sea.

Rain or shine

Water falls as rain, hail or snow, in a process called the water cycle. Some of it lands in lakes, rivers and streams. This is called surface water. Some water soaks into the ground, like water into a sponge. This is called groundwater.

The water companies take water from natural lakes and rivers. They also pump groundwater out of the rocks through deep wells called boreholes.

The water cycle

If you have watched a kettle boil you know that when water is heated it turns to steam. In the same way, when the sun warms the sea, lakes and rivers, the water turns into water vapour.

The water vapour rises into the air where it cools and forms tiny droplets of water again. We see these as clouds. Eventually the droplets join together and become too heavy to stay in the air. So they fall as rain, to fill rivers, lakes and the sea once again.

Clouds form

Rain falls to fill rivers and lakes

Water vapour rises into the air

The sun heats water forming water vapour

The rivers flow into the sea

A lot of rain water soaks into the ground

Pure, refreshing rain?

Rain water may look pure, but it isn't. As it falls it picks up dirt, dust and chemicals from the air. When it lands on the ground it collects mud, the remains of dead plants and small creatures, and tiny bacteria.

Water is also dirtied by humans and their activities. Farming causes soil, manure, fertilizers and pesticides to get into the water. Mining and other industries also introduce harmful chemicals into the water cycle.

So, before the water companies can supply water to our homes, it has to be carefully cleaned and treated.

WONDERFUL WATER

Your water bill

Water costs money. Storing, treating and supplying our water is expensive. Ask an adult the name of your local water company and how much your water bill is.

Severn Trent Water

Date
14 March 2000

Your account number
2638 8513 8576

Account enquiries call (at local call rate)
0845 7 500 500

You can call us 8.00 am to 8.00 pm Mondays to Fridays, and 8.00 am to 1.00 pm on Saturdays.

MR J SMITH 51329 516 /657
26 ACACIA AVENUE
NEWTOWN
SHROPSHIRE
NW4 123

Our address for payments by post has changed - please see overleaf for details

Water services bill

Rateable Value £87

Dear customer

This is your Water bill for the period 1 April 2000 to 31 March 2001.

The amount due is

£54.28

service	pence per £ RV	Charge (£)
Water Supply	62.40	£54.28

| Total payable | | £54.28 |

You can pay the total amount now using both payment slips or you can pay in two instalments.

| Amount due 1 April 2000 | £27.14 |
| Amount due 1 October 2000 | £27.14 |

The various ways to pay, including Direct Debit, are shown on the back of this bill.

Water treatment

River water is taken, via a pumping station, to a reservoir and then to a treatment plant.

Water in lakes, and groundwater is piped straight to the treatment works.

A pumping room at a treatment works

The quality of water varies according to its source. River water needs to pass through many stages of treatment. Groundwater doesn't usually need very much treatment.

Water is treated for several reasons. It has to be made clean and clear, with any dirt and bits removed. It must also have a pleasant taste and smell.

Water has to be made safe to drink, with all harmful germs and bacteria removed from it. The level of minerals in the water is also checked and adjusted.

WONDERFUL WATER

The first artificial reservoir

The world's first large artificial water reservoir was built at Panda Wewa in Colombia about 2500 years ago. It remained in use until the early nineteenth century.

Getting rid of the bits

The first stage in the water treatment process is 'screening'. Water is passed through coarse bar screens to remove large floating debris like logs and other objects. Then it passes through finer mesh screens to remove smaller objects like sticks and leaves.

After screening, water pours into large tanks.

Next the water is 'flocced'. It goes into a large tank where chemicals are added to it. These chemicals cause any tiny unwanted particles in the water to coagulate, or join together, to form what is called a 'floc'.

This woman is adjusting the chemicals that enter the tanks.

The floc forms a 'sludge blanket'. This solid sludge blanket is scraped off the surface or channelled off, loaded into skips and taken to a landfill site. Once the sludge blanket has been removed, the clean water is taken from the tank to be filtered.

Filtering and softening

Water is filtered by slowly passing it through silica sand or carbon to remove any remaining particles.

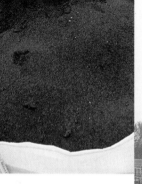

The carbon used for filtering (above)

The acidity and alkaline levels are checked and adjusted by adding chemicals to the water. Also the water is made 'softer'. Water that has lots of certain mineral salts in it is called 'hard' water. If very hard water was piped to your house, it would damage your pipes.

The tanks where the water is filtered

Lastly, the water is disinfected with chlorine which kills off any remaining bacteria. Chlorine is what you can smell in swimming baths.

At each stage, the water is tested to make sure that it is clean and safe. The clean water is then pumped into a covered storage reservoir.

Getting it to you

Storage reservoirs are often some way away from the people who need the water. So the water is piped to 'service reservoirs'. These are usually covered with grass and you can sometimes see them along the side of the road.

Most service reservoirs are on high ground, so that the water flows downhill and the companies don't have to pump it around. If you live in a really flat area or on the top of a hill, your water is probably stored in a water tower.

During the day water is piped from the reservoirs to houses, schools, offices and factories. It goes along mains pipes under the streets. The pipes that go into your house are as thick as a large hosepipe and are made of plastic.

At night, less water is used and the service reservoirs and water towers are refilled from the storage reservoir at the treatment works.

Water around the home

Most water mains pipes follow the road system. A branch pipe then carries water into your home. If you need to stop the water getting into the house there is a tap, or mains 'stopcock', to turn it all off.

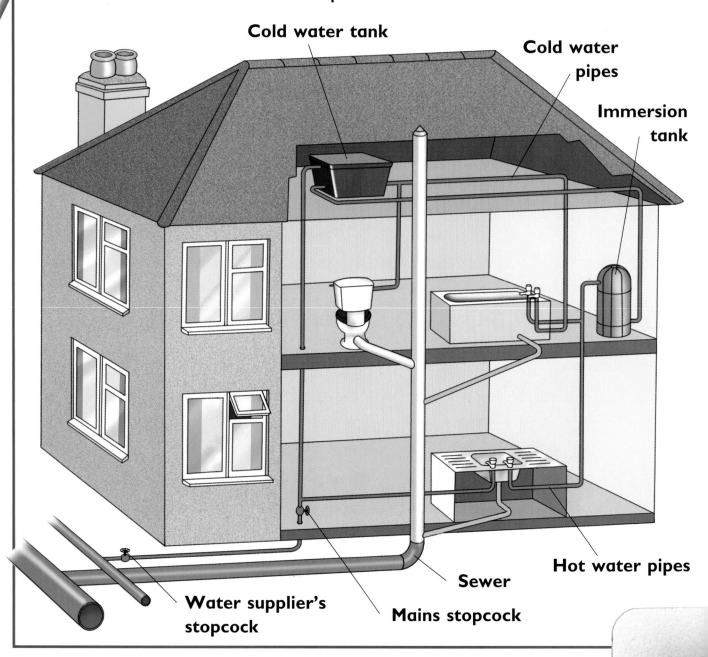

Cold water tank

Cold water pipes

Immersion tank

Hot water pipes

Sewer

Mains stopcock

Water supplier's stopcock

The water to your kitchen, and other places where water is needed for drinking or cooking, usually comes from the mains. Water going to the bathroom and for the central heating system is normally piped into tanks in the loft.

From there it flows down into the cold taps in the bathroom, or into the immersion tank, where it is heated for your hot water, or the radiators.

WONDERFUL WATER

Help! Burst pipe!

Water expands when it freezes. When this happens to the water in your pipes, they may burst and you will have a flood. This is why the pipes in your loft should be insulated with a thick layer of polystyrene to prevent the water in them freezing.

To the tap

There are pipes all over your house. The water makes its way from the tank in your loft, or from the hot water immersion tank, to the taps.

Immersion tanks are insulated to stop heat escaping.

A tap is an on/off switch. Inside it is a little rubber or plastic washer, which covers a hole. When you turn on the tap, the washer is moved away from the hole and water can flow. When you turn off the tap, the washer is moved to cover the hole again.

Probably most water in your house is used by flushing the toilet. Every time you flush, up to nine litres of water goes down the bowl. But where does it go then?

WONDERFUL WATER

Turn those taps off!

What would happen if you forgot to turn the taps off? If a tap were left on in a bathroom upstairs, it wouldn't be so long before the water overflowed out of the sink or bath, seeped into the carpets and floorboards, and through the ceiling. If water were to get into the electrical wiring system, it could cause a fire.

Down the plughole

The waste water that leaves your house is called sewage. It goes down into a sewer that is joined to an undergound sewerage system.

Here your waste water mixes with waste from other houses, shops and offices, travelling along bigger and bigger pipes.

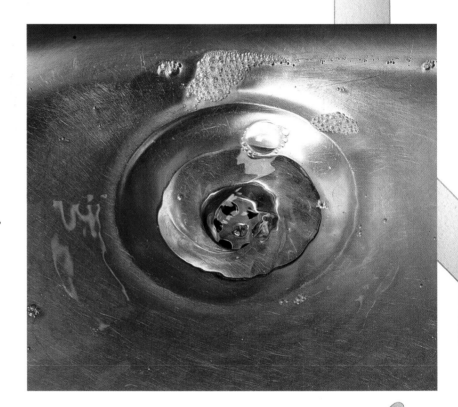

WONDERFUL WATER

How much water?

Think of a big bottle of lemonade – that's a litre. When you wash your face and hands you may use as much as nine litres of water, a shower uses 27 litres, a bath 90 litres and a washing machine 118 litres for each load.

Manhole covers in the street give sewerage workers access to the underground sewers so they can look after then.

In some rural areas, sewage goes to a septic tank. It is called a 'septic' tank because the water 'seeps' out of it into the surrounding ground. The solid waste left in the tank is collected by a road tanker and taken away for processing.

Sewage treatment

By the time sewage gets to a treatment works it is a souplike, dirty liquid, which contains food, detergents, human waste, oils, sand and perhaps even harmful chemicals. This all has to be cleaned and treated before it can be returned to the natural cycle.

In some ways, the process of treating sewage is quite similar to the treatment of water before it gets to our homes. First it is screened through metal screens to sieve out large objects such as wood, cans, bits of cloth and plastics.

Then it flows along wide channels, where any sand and grit sink to the bottom. From these channels, it passes to a settlement tank where the solid particles settle on the bottom and form 'sludge'. This sludge, in turn, is removed for treatment and disposal.

A settlement tank

WONDERFUL WATER

To the outhouse

Sewers were first laid in our cities at the end of the 1900s. Before then people threw their waste into the streets. They went to the toilet in little outhouses. Every so often 'night soil men' would come with their carts to remove the buckets from the outhouses. Not a pleasant job!

Back to the sea

The dirty liquid left at the top of the settlement tank has to be made clean and harmless.
This can be done in several ways.

One way is to sprinkle the liquid sewage over large, round beds of stones. Here the dirt in the liquid is eaten by billions of bacteria which cleans the liquid and greatly improves its quality.

The sludge left behind can be collected and made into fertilizer for farmers. However, in places where there is heavy industry the sludge may be full of dangerous chemicals. This kind of sludge is burned or deposited in landfill sites.

Water pollution

It is vital that rivers, streams and the sea are kept clean and free from harmful chemicals. Pollution by untreated sewage, farm or industrial waste can kill wildlife and harm our health too. Most water companies work closely with environmental groups and the Environment Agency to try to keep our water clean.

WONDERFUL WATER

Don't waste it!

There is the same amount of water in the world today as there was one million years ago. But, of course, there are many, many more people living here now, so there is less water to go around. Some parts of the world have much less rainfall than we do. This can cause drought and famine.

Even in Britain, there can be times when water is in short supply. Then we all have to be careful to use only the water we need. Here are some ways of saving water:

1. Use a watering can intead of a sprinkler, so that water gets only to the plants that need it. A sprinkler uses water at the rate of nine litres every minute.

2. Wash the car with a bucket and sponge instead of using a hosepipe.

3. Put a lemonade bottle filled with water, or even a brick, in your toilet cistern. This will mean that less water is used every time you flush.

You can also help the environment by using soap powders and washing-up liquids that are biodegradable. Biodegradable means that they will break down naturally in the environment.

Glossary

Acidity The level of acid, or sourness, of something. Acidity is measured on a scale known as the pH scale which goes from 0 to 14. Our water is treated to have an acidity level of 7. If the pH level is above this, it is considered to be too alkaline.

Bacteria Very, very tiny living things that can be harmful.

Carbon The main element in charcoal and other forms of coal.

Debris Bits of rubbish, stones, wood and other materials.

Disinfecting The use of a substance to kill germs.

Fertilizers The materials spread on soil to improve its quality and make it more productive.

Insulate To wrap with protective material to keep from freezing.

Landfill site The place where people's rubbish is taken when it has been collected from homes, shops and offices.

Minerals Naturally-occurring chemical elements or compounds. Minerals are found in the soil, and rocks are made up of mixtures of minerals.

Particles The tiny parts of which everything is made.

Pesticides Chemicals used to kill insects and pests.

Reservoir An artificial, or man-made lake, for storing water.

Skips The large metal containers in which big items of rubbish, rubble, wood and other waste are collected.

Untreated sewage Sewage that hasn't been processed at a sewage treatment works. It is also known as raw sewage.

Water vapour The invisible moisture in the air.

Further reading

Jervis, Paola, *Water*, Franklin Watts, 1996
Manning, Mick, *Splish splash splosh!*, Franklin Watts, 1996
Perham, Molly, *Water*, Franklin Watts, 1996
Ramsay, Helena, *Water*, Franklin Watts, 1998

Further information

Severn Trent, who helped with the production of this book, supplies top quality tap water to seven million people every day, and protects the environment from the waste water of 3.5 million homes and businesses across the Midlands.

Severn Trent runs a number of Education Centres across the Midlands which cater for visiting schools free of charge. Below is a list of three centres:

Stoke Bardolph Education Centre
Stoke Lane
Stoke Bardolph
Burton Joyce
Nottingham
NG14 5HL
Tel: 0115 961 6504

Cropston Education Centre
Bradgate Road
Cropston
Leicester
LE7 7GB
Tel: 0116 235 2014

Minworth Education Centre
Kingsbury Road
Minworth
Birmingham
B76 9DP
Tel: 0121 313 2027

For other sources of information about the water industry, contact the industry organization, Water UK, which has a website (www.water.org.uk) with information about, and links to, all the regional water companies. You can also contact them at:

1 Queen Anne's Gate
London SW1H 9BT
Tel: 020 7344 1844

Index

Plants on the attack

Some plants don't make all of their food by photosynthesis, but get it in other ways. Parasitic plants, such as mistletoe, grow on other plants and absorb food and water from them. Some eventually end up killing the plant they are living on, while others live alongside the plant they live on.

A few plants actually get their food by trapping and killing animals and absorbing energy and nutrients from them. These plants are called carnivorous plants. Pitcher plants, sticky sundews, and Venus flytraps are all carnivorous.

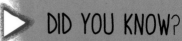

DID YOU KNOW?

Some pitcher plants in the Philippines are large enough to trap and eat rats! Around one metre (3 feet) wide, these plants have cup-shaped parts filled with liquid. Any animal climbing on the plant can easily fall into these slippery cups, and cannot escape.

This sundew has trapped a fly with the sticky liquid on its hairs.

Our amazing world of plants

Plants really are amazing – they take the Sun's energy and change it into food to fuel their growth. They also provide food for lots of animals, including humans. To do this, they need the right conditions for germination: warmth, oxygen, and water. Once they have grown into seedlings, they need sunlight, water, and nutrients to grow into larger plants. Then they can produce flowers. If these flowers get pollinated, the plants can make seeds and these can grow into new plants.

Leaves are the factories of Earth – they capture sunlight and turn it into food.

▷ DID YOU KNOW?
Bamboo is the fastest-growing plant - it can grow up to 1 metre (3 feet) per day! Bamboo is actually a type of grass. People have used it for hundreds of years, for fishing, papermaking, gardening, crafts, buildings, and weapons.

Plants across the world

Plants grow in almost every **habitat** on Earth, from the frozen thin soils in the Arctic to the lush green forests of the Amazon. Wherever they grow, they have adapted to be able to survive there. They make it possible for many animals to live in these habitats too, because without plants to provide food and shelter, there would be very few animals.

Animals rely on plants to provide them with food and shelter.

Eureka moment!

Between 1803 and 1806, Meriwether Lewis and William Clark explored a route through the west and north-west of America. Along the way, they discovered almost 200 new plants!

43

Glossary

absorb soak up

adaptation feature of a living thing that has changed over time to suit the environment

camouflage colour or shape that blends in with the background

carbon dioxide colourless, odourless gas found in the air

cell tiny unit that makes up all parts of plants. Different plant parts are made of different kinds of cells.

chlorophyll green substance in plant leaves and stems that traps sunlight for photosynthesis

food chain series of living things where each one is eaten by the next

germination process by which seeds find conditions favourable and start to grow into new plants

habitat natural environment of an animal or plant

herbivore animal that feeds on plants

nectar sweet liquid made by plants to attract animals. When the animals eat the nectar, they gather pollen which they can then take to another flower.

nerve long fibre in an animal's body that carries messages to and from different parts

nutrient chemical that helps plants to live and grow

ovary part of a flower that contains the ovule

ovule part of a flower that contains the female cells. This develops into a seed when it is fertilized.

photosynthesis process by which plants use water, sunlight, and carbon dioxide to make food for themselves

pollen fine powder made in the flowers of plants that is used by plants to fertilize flowers and make seeds

pollination process by which male plant cells, carried in pollen, land on female parts of the flower

reproduce join with another living thing of the same species to make offspring

root plant part that usually grows under the ground. Roots hold the plant up, and take in water and nutrients.

sap liquid inside a plant that contains water and nutrients

season one of the times of the year. In some parts of the world, spring, summer, autumn, and winter are seasons. Other parts of the world may have wet and dry seasons.

shoot new growth on a plant; after the root, it is the first bit of a plant to grow from a germinated seed

species type of living thing that can breed with another of the same species to produce offspring

spore tiny particle produced by some plants. Spores grow into tiny plants that can then be fertilized to make new plants like the parent plant.

stamen male part of flowers that makes pollen

stem main part of a plant that supports the branches, leaves, and flowers

stigma female part of a flower where pollen can land and travel to meet the ovule

stomata microscopic holes in plant leaves. Water and gases can pass in and out of stomata.

Find out more

Books

Experiments with Plants (My Science Investigations), Christine Taylor-Butler (Raintree, 2011)

Plant Reproduction (Sci-Hi), Barbara A. Somervill (Raintree, 2009)

Plants (Science Library), Peter Riley (Miles Kelly Publishing, 2009)

Plants (Super Science), Richard Robinson (QED Publishing, 2007)

Websites

www.bbc.co.uk/bitesize/ks2/science/living_things

This BBC Bitesize website has sections on plants and plant life cycles. Each section has information you can read, and activities and quizzes to test yourself.

www.bbc.co.uk/nature/plants

This website has lots of information about plants. There are also some amazing film clips of plants all around the world.

www.kew.org/learn/kids/index.htm

The website for the Royal Botanical Gardens in Kew, Surrey, has a section for children. There are video clips and ideas for things to do and make at home, as well as instructions for joining in "The Great Plant Hunt".

ntbg.org/plants/index.php

On Hawaii's National Tropical Botanical Garden website, you can find out about tropical plants. There is a "kids' corner" where you can take a virtual tour and try some puzzles.

www.sciencekids.co.nz/plants.html

You can play games on this website, learn about how plants grow, and find out about the life cycle of plants. There are also some videos to watch – you can see Venus flytraps catching insects!

Organizations

Wild About Plants

www.wildaboutplants.org.uk

This organization's website is all about the wild plants growing in the UK. You can look at habitat guides to see what kinds of plants you might expect to find in areas near you. You can take part in surveys to see which flowers grow in your area. They provide useful information about poisonous flowers, too!

WWF

www.wwf.org.uk

This organization was set up in 1961. It aims to protect the diversity of plants and animals around the world. It campaigns for less pollution and better use of resources, and other ways of reducing the human impact on Earth.

Further research

Natural History Museum

Cromwell Road
London SW7 5BD
www.nhm.ac.uk

The Natural History Museum has many displays and activities to demonstrate the amazing diversity of life on Earth. You can learn about how plants and animals have changed over time, and how scientists work to discover all about the natural world.

Royal Botanic Gardens, Kew

26 West Park Road
Richmond
Surrey TW9 4DA
www.kew.org

The Royal Botanic Gardens in Kew has collections of plant species from all over the world. The researchers there work to conserve plants. They have created the Millennium Seed Bank in Wakehurst, Sussex, and there they store the seeds of 10 per cent of the world's plants. They aim to have collected 25 per cent by 2020.

The Eden Project

Bodelva
St Austell
Cornwall PL24 2SG
ww.edenproject.com

The Eden Project is a series of huge domed greenhouses, one of which contains a rainforest! You can wander through lots of different biomes and look at the plants that grow there. There are fun activities and amazing things to learn about plants.

Go for a walk in your local nature park! Spend time looking closely at all the different plants you can see. Can you identify any of them?

Index